Elementary

ENGLISH STREAM

Osamu Takeuchi   Seijiro Sumi   Tomoko Yabukoshi
Michiko Ueki   Brent Cotsworth

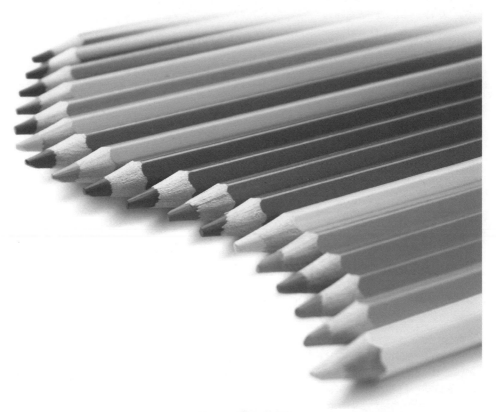

KINSEIDO

Kinseido Publishing Co., Ltd.
3-21 Kanda Jimbo-cho, Chiyoda-ku,
Tokyo 101-0051, Japan

Copyright © 2019 by Osamu Takeuchi
　　　　　　　　　Seijiro Sumi
　　　　　　　　　Tomoko Yabukoshi
　　　　　　　　　Michiko Ueki
　　　　　　　　　Brent Cotsworth

All rights reserved. No part of this publication may be reproduced, stored in a retrieval system, or transmitted, in any form or by any means, electronic, mechanical, photocopying, recording or otherwise, without the prior permission of the publisher.

First published 2019 by Kinseido Publishing Co., Ltd.

Design:　sein
Editorial support: Ai Okasaka

Texts:
Units 2, 8, & 12　　Anthony Allan
Units 6, 10, & 15　Kevin Cleary
Units 1, 11, & 14　Michael Hood
Units 3, 5, & 13　　Braven Smillie
Units 4, 7, & 9　　Mark D. Stafford

Photo:
p. 15　©Incredible Edible Todmorden

音声ファイル無料ダウンロード

http://www.kinsei-do.co.jp/download/4079

この教科書で 🎧 DL 00 の表示がある箇所の音声は、上記 URL または QR コードにて無料でダウンロードできます。自習用音声としてご活用ください。

- ▶ PC からのダウンロードをお勧めします。スマートフォンなどでダウンロードされる場合は、**ダウンロード前に「解凍アプリ」をインストール**してください。
- ▶ URL は、**検索ボックスではなくアドレスバー (URL 表示欄) に入力**してください。
- ▶ お使いのネットワーク環境によっては、ダウンロードできない場合があります。

◎ CD 00 ▶ 左記の表示がある箇所の音声は、教室用 CD（Class Audio CD）に収録されています。

はじめに

　本書 *English Stream: Elementary* は、ご好評を頂いている *Reading Stream: Elementary* の題材を基盤にしつつ、そこに発信と技能統合の要素を新たに取り入れ、英語運用能力を総合的に育成していくことを企図して編まれた教科書です。

　本書の中核となる **Reading** の読み物（各 Unit 300 語程度）は、5 名の英語ネイティブ話者による書き下ろしテキストを採用し、このレベルの学習者が出会うと考えられる様々なジャンルで書かれた、興味をそそるトピックの文章で構成するようにしました。また、テキストの語彙は、各種語彙リストを参照して、2,000 語レベルに設定されています。

　Unit の冒頭では、それぞれの Unit の目的（めあて）が明示されており、到達点が見えるような工夫がなされています。その後の **Pre-reading tasks A** および **B** では、読み物と関連する話題について、自分の考えを短く述べる活動や、他の人の意見を聞く活動、さらにはクラスメイトと意見を交換したりする活動が導入されています。英語でのやり取りを通して、背景知識の活性化と、意見交換への積極的姿勢の涵養が図れるよう活動をデザインしてみました。

　Reading の本文テキストは、重要語句を太字にするだけで、側注など注意を散漫にする要素を末尾にまとめ、読むことに集中できるようにしてあります。また、**Notes** では、2,000 語レベルを超えた語彙や固有名詞などが、リーディングの際に目障りにならないように提示されています。なお、**Reading** の末尾には、「読み方のコツ」を簡潔かつ明示的に提示しました。これを通して、学習者が読解ストラテジー（読み方）への認識を高め、様々な読み方にチャレンジしてくれるよう、期待を込めて作成しました。さらに、本文テキストを読み上げた音声 CD も用意されていますので、シャドーイングや音読練習に活用されることをお薦めします。加えて、学習者の自学用に、金星堂のウェブサイトからダウンロードしてお使いいただける音声ファイルも用意しました（左ページ下の説明をご参照ください）。

　本文テキストを読み終わると、内容理解から発信へと深化していく **Post-reading tasks** で学習することになります。まず、**Post-reading tasks A** では、テキスト構造の理解を助けるグラフィック・オーガナイザーを使って学びます。グラフィック・オーガナイザーの空所を埋めていくことで、テキスト構造の見取り図が現れてくる仕組みになっています。次に、**Post-reading tasks B** では、T/F 形式で内容理解に間違いがないかを確認します。T/F の 2 択では偶然に正解する

危険性も上がるため、ここでは本文中の根拠となる文章を指摘する形式を採用しています。この **Post-reading tasks A** と **Post-reading tasks B** の構成は、テキストを一回だけ読むのではなく、概要から細部へというように視点を変えて、複数回読むことを奨励する意図のもとに作られています。

　締めくくりの **Post-reading tasks C** では、発信につながる様々な活動が提供されています。段階を追いながら、自分が見聞きしたものや自分の考えを、自らのコトバ（英語）で表現する力が養えるように活動をデザインしてみました。いきなり英語で表現するのは困難でも、**Pre-reading tasks** で背景知識を活性化し、意見を交換する姿勢を養い、**Reading** と **Post-reading tasks** で内容知識を入れ、表現を学んだ後では、ハードルも下がるはずです。無理だと諦めずに、この **Post-reading tasks C** を十分に活用して、各 **Unit** のまとめとしての「発信する力」を伸ばしていって欲しいものです。

　以上のように、様々な工夫をこらした本書での学習を通して、学習者のみなさんが英語運用能力をバランスよく伸ばしていかれることを、編著者一同、祈ってやみません。

　最後になりましたが、本書の完成にご尽力いただきました金星堂編集部のみなさんに、心よりお礼を申し上げます。

2019 年初冬
竹内　　理
住　政二郎
薮越　知子
植木美千子
Brent Cotsworth

CONTENTS

UNIT 1 | **To Drive or to Ride?**
トピックセンテンスとパラグラフの構造を理解する ………… 11

UNIT 2 | **Help Yourselves**
原因と結果を述べる ………………………………………… 15

UNIT 3 | **What I Learned from Fay**
経験を語る（物語）………………………………………… 19

UNIT 4 | **Ways to Help Others**
分類しながら説明する ……………………………………… 23

UNIT 5 | **Can Fish Fall from the Sky?!**
報告する（時事ニュース）………………………………… 27

UNIT 6 | **How to Prepare for a Presentation**
手順を説明する ……………………………………………… 31

UNIT 7 | **International Date Line**
事実を時系列に沿って説明する …………………………… 35

UNIT 8 | **What Is Friendship?**
定義を示して例示する ……………………………………… 39

UNIT 9	Entering a Photo Contest

効率的に情報を伝える (e-mail) ……………………………………… 43

UNIT 10	Getting Money for a Big Project

比較する ………………………………………………………………… 47

UNIT 11	Accepting the "Salesperson of the Year" Award

スピーチの文体に慣れる ……………………………………………… 51

UNIT 12	Written Art

コミュニケーションのスタイルを理解する ………………………… 55

UNIT 13	Life Advice Q & A with Dr. Joyce Green

目的をもって尋ねる(人生相談)……………………………………… 59

UNIT 14	The Economy Is Strong, for Now

経済記事を読んでグラフを完成させる ……………………………… 63

UNIT 15	Not Hearing a Gorilla

報告する(科学)……………………………………………………… 67

記録シート ……………………………………………………………… 9

*小テストの結果を記録して提出しましょう

Recording Sheet for Review Quizzes（半期授業用）

Student ID: | Name:

Unit 1	Unit 2	Unit 3	Unit 4	Unit 5
/10	/10	/10	/10	/10
Unit 6	Unit 7	Unit 8	Unit 9	Unit 10
/10	/10	/10	/10	/10
Unit 11	Unit 12	Unit 13	Unit 14	Unit 15
/10	/10	/10	/10	/10

Total of All Units **/150**

······切り取り線······

Recording Sheet for Review Quizzes（通年授業用）

Student ID: | Name:

Unit 1		Unit 2		Unit 3		Unit 4		Unit 5	
Type A	Type B	Type A	Type B	Type A	Type B	Type A	Type B	Type A	Type B
/10	/10	/10	/10	/10	/10	/10	/10	/10	/10
Unit 6		Unit 7		Unit 8		Unit 9		Unit 10	
Type A	Type B	Type A	Type B	Type A	Type B	Type A	Type B	Type A	Type B
/10	/10	/10	/10	/10	/10	/10	/10	/10	/10
Unit 11		Unit 12		Unit 13		Unit 14		Unit 15	
Type A	Type B	Type A	Type B	Type A	Type B	Type A	Type B	Type A	Type B
/10	/10	/10	/10	/10	/10	/10	/10	/10	/10

Total of All Units **/300**

UNIT 1

To Drive or to Ride?

トピックセンテンスとパラグラフの構造を理解する

このユニットでは、公共交通機関の利用に関する文章を通して、トピックセンテンス*とパラグラフの構造について学びます。

* 主題文のこと。著者がそのパラグラフで論じようとしていることを要約した1文。

Pre-reading tasks

A 自分の意見に合うものを [ ] から選ぶか ( ) に記入して、質問に答えましょう。

Q1. Which do you think is better, using public transportation or owning a car?
▶ I think it is better to [**use public transportation** / **own a car**].

Q2. Why do you think so?
▶ Because it is [**cheaper** / **safer** / **better for the environment** / **more convenient** / (　　　　　　　　)].

B **A** のQ1〜2について、クラスメイトの意見を聞いてみましょう。

	Peer #1 Name: _____	Peer #2 Name: _____
Q1.	☐ use public transportation ☐ own a car	☐ use public transportation ☐ own a car
Q2.	☐ cheaper ☐ safer ☐ better for the environment ☐ more convenient ☐ (　　　　　　　　)	☐ cheaper ☐ safer ☐ better for the environment ☐ more convenient ☐ (　　　　　　　　)

11

次の英文を読みましょう（太字は本 Unit の重要語句です）。

To Drive or to Ride?

1 If you live in a big city, you may find that it is better to use public transportation than to own a car. This is because trains and buses are cheaper, safer, and better for the environment than cars. First, owning a car is **expensive**. You must **pay** not only for the car, but also for the fuel, repairs, and parking.
5 When all the costs are added up, public transportation is almost always much **cheaper**. Second, taking public transportation is safer than driving a car. Although bus and train accidents do happen, they are rare, and they do not often result in **serious** injury. However, car accidents happen every day, and they sometimes cause serious injury or even death. Finally, buses and trains
10 use far less energy than cars. This helps to keep the air clean. Although most cars use less fuel than buses, they often **carry** only one person. One bus, on the other hand, can carry 75 people or more. Energy use **per person** is much less for people who ride the bus. Trains are even more efficient, carrying hundreds of people **at a time**. Therefore, if you want to save money, stay safe, and save
15 energy, public transportation is the way to go.

2 If you live in the countryside, however, a car might be a better choice. Public transportation only **makes sense** in areas where many people live and work. **What if** you can't get to a bus or train stop within a few minutes? What if the bus or train cannot get you to where you are going within a short period of
20 time? In such cases, a car makes more sense. Also, public transportation is not **energy-efficient** if only a few people use it. This is why you will not see as many buses or trains outside of big cities.

Notes

l. 1: public transportation「公共交通機関」 l. 4: fuel「燃料」 l. 5: add up「〜を加算する」 l. 7: rare「めったにない、まれな」 l. 8: result in「〜の結果となる」 l. 8: injury「怪我」 l. 13: efficient「効率的な」

UNIT 1 To Drive or to Ride?

> **読み方のコツ**
>
> トピックセンテンスは、パラグラフの先頭にあることが多く、文章全体の内容を理解するために大切な情報が含まれているので注意しましょう。

Post-reading tasks

A 本文の内容をもとにして以下の図を完成させましょう。

第1パラグラフのトピックセンテンス：

都市では車よりも（1. 　　　　　　　）が便利

- 公共交通機関の方がより（2. 　　　　　　　）
- 公共交通機関の方がより（3. 　　　　　　　）
- 公共交通機関の方がより消費エネルギーが（4. 　　　　　　　）

第2パラグラフのトピックセンテンス：

田舎では公共交通機関よりも（5. 　　　　　　　）が便利

- バス停や駅が家の近くにあるとは限らない
- 目的地に着くまでに時間がかかる
- たった数人しか公共交通機関を利用しない場合、（6. 　　　　　　　）が悪くなる
　　→田舎で多くのバスや電車を目にしない理由

B 次の各文が本文の内容に合っていればT、間違っていればFを（　）に記入しましょう。また、その根拠となった本文中の文に下線を引きましょう。

1. (　) People living in a big city can save money if they use public transportation.
2. (　) Driving a car is safer than taking a public bus.
3. (　) Using public transportation helps reduce air pollution in a city.
4. (　) A bus can carry more people at one time than a train.
5. (　) Owning a car might be convenient for people living in the countryside.

> パラグラフは、多くの場合、主題のトピックセンテンスから始まり、その後にトピックセンテンスを支える複数のサポートセンテンスが続き、まとまりのある意味を構成します。サポートセンテンスでは、主題を支持する理由や例などが述べられます。各サポートセンテンスが自然につながっていることも大切です。パラグラフの最後は「まとめ」にあたるコンクルーディングセンテンスで終わります。以下の例で確認してみましょう。
>
> **e.g.**
> Tom is a very hardworking student. He wakes up at five every morning and studies two hours before class starts. He always hands in his reports and always gets As. We believe that he will receive a scholarship from the university.

1. 以下のトピックセンテンスを支持するサポートセンテンスを2つ日本語で書きましょう。コンクルーディングセンテンスは変更してもかまいません。

    トピックセンテンス：海外旅行に行くことは、人生を豊かにしてくれます。

    サポートセンテンスA：＿＿＿＿＿＿＿＿＿＿＿＿＿＿＿＿＿＿＿＿＿＿＿＿＿＿

    サポートセンテンスB：＿＿＿＿＿＿＿＿＿＿＿＿＿＿＿＿＿＿＿＿＿＿＿＿＿＿

    コンクルーディングセンテンス：（こうした経験は、将来のために自信になるでしょう。）
    ＿＿＿＿＿＿＿＿＿＿＿＿＿＿＿＿＿＿＿＿＿＿＿＿

2. 1で書いたサポートセンテンスを英語にして、パラグラフを完成させましょう。コンクルーディングセンテンスは変更してもかまいません。

    Topic sentence: Traveling abroad makes our life richer.

    Supporting sentence A: ＿＿＿＿＿＿＿＿＿＿＿＿＿＿＿＿＿＿＿＿＿

    Supporting sentence B: ＿＿＿＿＿＿＿＿＿＿＿＿＿＿＿＿＿＿＿＿＿

    Concluding sentence: (These experiences will give us confidence in the future.)
    ＿＿＿＿＿＿＿＿＿＿＿＿＿＿＿＿＿＿＿＿＿＿＿＿

UNIT 2

Help Yourselves

原因と結果を述べる

このユニットでは、地域の活動について書かれた文章を通して、原因と結果を述べる方法を学びます。

🫘 Pre-reading tasks

A 自分の意見に合うものを [ ] から選ぶか ( ) に記入して、質問に答えましょう。

Q1. Have you ever participated in any volunteer activities?　▶ [Yes. / No.]

Q2. What kind of social issues are you interested in?
　　▶ I am interested in [educational / environmental / economic /
　　(　　　　　　　　)] issues.

B A の Q1〜2 について、クラスメイトの意見を聞いてみましょう。

	Peer #1 Name: _____	Peer #2 Name: _____
Q1.	☐ Yes.　☐ No. → If yes, what kind of activities? (　　　　　　　　　　　　)	☐ Yes.　☐ No. → If yes, what kind of activities? (　　　　　　　　　　　　)
Q2.	☐ educational　☐ environmental ☐ economic　　☐ (　　　　　)	☐ educational　☐ environmental ☐ economic　　☐ (　　　　　)

15

Help Yourselves

1 This is the story of how one challenge changed a town. Todmorden is a small town in Yorkshire, England. One day, Pam, a lady who lived in the town, **attended** a **conference** on climate change. At the conference, a professor said that people should try to be responsible for the food they ate, and **urged** the audience to grow food themselves. This was the challenge he put to them.

2 On her way home, Pam thought about the professor's words. Was it possible for her town to produce and **rely on** food grown there? Would the local people be interested in doing this? She discussed the idea with a friend, Mary, who was so excited about it that she decided to plant vegetables in her front garden. As the vegetables grew and ripened, she put a sign in the garden that said: "Help Yourselves." This created a lot of discussion in the town. A greater effect was that it encouraged other people to start growing vegetables, too.

3 As interest grew, members of the community **volunteered** to clear waste ground around the town. Then they built soil beds there and planted vegetables. They also planted trees in the town and started a campaign to encourage everyone to eat local eggs. Some people even bought and kept hens to **lay** them! All of Todmorden's schools participated in the movement, too. The high school even built an eco-friendly **fish farm**.

4 People from all over the UK and even from abroad traveled to Todmorden to **observe** this wonderful example of **positive change** in the community. Even Prince Charles wanted to learn about it, so he visited the town to see for himself. He could see that helping others means helping yourself. Pam and Mary must **be proud of** their achievements and their town.

Notes

l. 1: Todmorden「トッドモーデン」（イングランド北部ヨークシャーに位置する人口約1万2千人の街）
l. 10: ripen「熟する」 l. 10: Help Yourselves「どうぞお食べください」 l. 14: soil beds「苗床」（四方を木の板などで囲み肥沃な土を入れて作ったもの） l. 16: hens「めんどり」 l. 17: participate in「〜に参加する」

UNIT 2 Help Yourselves

読み方のコツ

原因と結果を含む文章では、最初に原因が述べられ、次に結果（あるいはその逆）が書かれています。何が原因で、どのような結果につながったのかに注意して読みましょう。

Post-reading tasks

A 本文の内容をもとにして以下の図を完成させましょう。

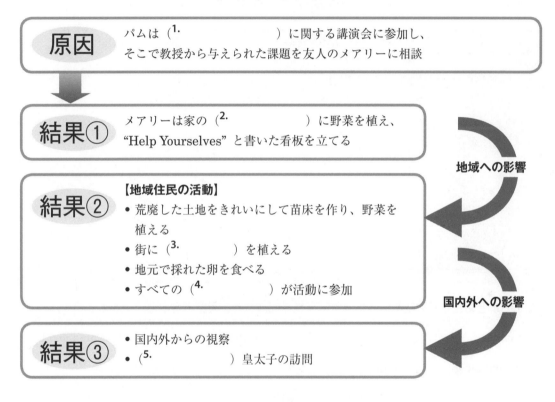

B 次の各文が本文の内容に合っていればT、間違っていればFを（ ）に記入しましょう。また、その根拠となった本文中の文に下線を引きましょう。

1. (　) Pam gave a talk at a conference on climate change.
2. (　) A friend of Pam's started growing flowers at school.
3. (　) The message on the board encouraged people in the town to start growing food.
4. (　) One high school started growing fish.
5. (　) The positive changes in Todmorden only drew attention from people in the community.

c

1. 以下の社会問題から 1 つを選び、その原因を 2 点調べて日本語と英語でまとめましょう。選択肢以外の社会問題を選んでもかまいません。

地球温暖化（global warming）　　通勤ラッシュ（commuter rush hour）

歩きスマホ（texting while walking）　　高齢化社会（aging society）

過疎化（depopulation）　　教育格差（educational inequity）

	Japanese	English
【社会問題】		
【原因 1】		
【原因 2】		

2. 1 でまとめた内容を空所に書き入れて英文を完成させ、英語で発表してみましょう。

I chose _____ as my topic because it has become

a serious social problem.

（私は、深刻な社会問題になっている【社会問題】を選びました。）

I think that one possible cause is (that) _____

_____.

（考えられる 1 つの原因は、【原因 1】だと思います。）

Another possible cause is (that) _____

_____.

（考えられるもう 1 つの原因は、【原因 2】だと思います。）

UNIT 3

What I Learned from Fay

経験を語る（物語）

このユニットでは、恐怖症を克服した経験について書かれた文章を通して、経験を物語る方法を学びます。

Pre-reading tasks

A 自分の意見に合うものを［ ］から選ぶか（ ）に記入して、質問に答えましょう。

Q1. Do you worry a lot?　▶ [**Yes.** / **No.**]

Q2. What are you afraid of?
▶ I am afraid of [**dogs** / **cats** / **water** / **high places** / (　　　　　　)].

B Ａ の Q1 ～ 2 について、クラスメイトの意見を聞いてみましょう。

	Peer #1 Name: _____	Peer #2 Name: _____
Q1.	☐ Yes. ☐ No.	☐ Yes. ☐ No.
Q2.	☐ dogs　☐ cats　☐ water ☐ high places　☐ (　　　　)	☐ dogs　☐ cats　☐ water ☐ high places　☐ (　　　　)

Reading

次の英文を読みましょう（太字は本 Unit の重要語句です）。

What I Learned from Fay

1 When I was young, I was **afraid of** high places. In a tall building, I couldn't go near the windows. When the scary feeling came, my legs became **weak**. My mouth became dry. My hands shook. My heart beat quickly. And I was unable to talk.

2 Now let me tell you about my little sister, Fay. She is seven years younger than me, and I have always loved her very much. When she was two years old, she was starting to walk. She **liked to** look at new things, touch them and show them to me. One day, we were at a friend's house. We were watching TV, and Fay, as always, was looking at and touching everything around her.

3 I looked behind us, and saw Fay. She had **climbed on** a table by an open window, and she was standing in the window. My friend lived in a tall building, and that window was more than 100 feet **above the ground**. **Fear** came as I watched Fay stand there, smiling at me. I wanted to **scream**. But if I did, it might have made her move and **fall out of** the window. I walked slowly to the window. I shook as I felt the fear. But I couldn't show it to Fay. She might move. I went to the window and **pulled** Fay inside. Then she was safe, and that made me feel good.

4 Next, I looked out the window, and felt something new. I wasn't afraid anymore. I looked down at the cars and people. But my legs weren't shaking.

Since that day, I have never been afraid of high places. My love for Fay made me go to the window. It made me **face** my fear. And now I know that love is stronger than fear. Thank you, Fay!

Notes

l. 2: scary「怖い、おそろしい」 l. 10: look behind「〜の後ろをふりかえる」
l. 12: feet「フィート」(1 フィート＝約 30.5 cm)

UNIT 3 What I Learned from Fay

> **読み方のコツ**
>
> 物語を読むときには、「登場人物」、「場面」、「展開」、そして「結末」などを整理しながら読むとよいでしょう。

Post-reading tasks

A 本文の内容をもとにして以下の表を完成させましょう。

登場人物	私(語り手)：幼いころ(¹.　　　　　　　)が苦手だった フェイ(妹)：私よりも(².　　)歳年下
場面	友達の家：高い建物の中にあり、窓は地上から(³.　　　　) 　　　　　以上も高いところにある
何がおこった？	窓辺にフェイが立っていた。私は、窓辺に近づき、部屋の中に彼女を引きこんだ
物語の結末	その経験以来、私は、高いところを(⁴.　　　　)と感じることはなくなった

B 次の各文が本文の内容に合っていればT、間違っていればFを(　)に記入しましょう。また、その根拠となった本文中の文に下線を引きましょう。

1. (　) When the narrator was in a tall place, her legs turned weak.
2. (　) Fay started walking when she was three years old.
3. (　) When Fay climbed on the table, the window was closed.
4. (　) The narrator screamed when she saw her sister.
5. (　) The narrator's legs were shaking after she pulled Fay inside the room.

C

1. 以下の例を参考に、思い出に残っていることについてメモを完成させましょう。

e.g.

Who	Me
When	the second year of high school
What	I was a member of the soccer club.
Why	We won the final match and became the champions of the Tokyo league.

Who	
When	
What	
Why	

2. 1のメモと以下の例を参考にして、思い出について書いてみましょう。

e.g.

When I was in the second year of high school, I was a member of the soccer club. We won the final match and became the champions of the Tokyo league. This is one of the things I remember the most.

_____
_____
_____
_____
_____

UNIT 4

Ways to Help Others

分類しながら説明する

> このユニットでは、人助けの方法が紹介された文章を通して、分類しながら説明する方法を学びます。

🍃 Pre-reading tasks

A 自分の意見に合うものを [ ] から選ぶか（ ）に記入して、質問に答えましょう。

Q1. Have you ever helped someone before? ▶ [**Yes.** / **No.**]

Q2. How would you like to help others?
   ▶ I am interested in helping others by offering extra [**money** / **food** / **time** / (　　　　　　　)].

B AのQ1〜2について、クラスメイトの意見を聞いてみましょう。

	Peer #1 Name: _____	Peer #2 Name: _____
Q1.	☐ Yes. ☐ No. → If yes, how? (　　　　　　　　　　)	☐ Yes. ☐ No. → If yes, how? (　　　　　　　　　　)
Q2.	☐ money ☐ food ☐ time ☐ (　　　　　　　　)	☐ money ☐ food ☐ time ☐ (　　　　　　　　)

Ways to Help Others

1 Perhaps the biggest reason for the **remarkable** success of the human species is that we help each other like no other form of life. We cooperate very well in business, sports, and education on a daily basis, but perhaps the finest time we help others is when people are in need. There are three basic ways that individuals can help others. All of them have different **benefits** but each is quite **rewarding**.

2 Giving money is perhaps the easiest and most common way to help others. This form of giving is as easy as dropping extra change into an **aid** box at a convenience store. Usually, an aid group collects funds for either general or specific purposes and delivers the money to those in need. To **encourage** giving, some governments may even **offer** tax breaks for people who hand over large amounts to charities.

3 Another way to help others is to give **unneeded** items like extra food, second-hand clothing, or even used cars to an aid group. The charity then passes the goods on to people with specific needs directly or might sell a large piece of **property** and then give the funds to needy people. People who give away property may also enjoy tax breaks.

4 A third way to help others is to volunteer time. This can be **delivering** food, cleaning houses, helping build things, or teaching skills and languages. Although volunteering time is much harder than offering money or goods, and there are usually no tax breaks for doing so, it is **without a doubt** the most rewarding way to help others.

5 Giving money, property, or time to others are wonderful things to do. While the rewards of getting tax breaks, gaining personal pride, or receiving happiness might encourage us to give, simply helping others in need is always a good thing.

Notes

l. 2: like no other「他の〜と違って」 l. 2: form of life「生命、生物」 l. 4: in need「必要としている、困っている」 l. 11: tax breaks「税控除、減税」 l. 11: hand over「〜を引き渡す、譲与する」

UNIT 4 Ways to Help Others

読み方のコツ

分類しながら説明する文章では、パラグラフごとに、ひとつの分類の事例や特徴が述べられていくものです。パラグラフごとに関連する情報を整理しながら読むとよいでしょう。

Post-reading tasks

A 本文の内容をもとにして以下の図を完成させましょう。

個人がおこなう人助けの方法 とてもやり甲斐のあるすばらしいこと

1. お金を寄付する
   例：コンビニで余ったお釣りを（1.　　　　）に入れる

2. 不要な物を（2.　　　　　）に送る
   例：余った（3.　　　　）、古着、（4.　　　　）を送る

3. 自分の時間をボランティアに費やす
   例：（3.　　　　）を届けたり、家の（5.　　　　）をしたりする

B 次の各文が本文の内容に合っていればT、間違っていればFを（　）に記入しましょう。また、その根拠となった本文中の文に下線を引きましょう。

1. (　) Individuals help each other in business, sports, and education.

2. (　) This article presents five basic ways to help others.

3. (　) In many cases, individuals give money directly to people in need.

4. (　) If individuals offer their property, they may get tax breaks.

5. (　) It is easier to volunteer time than to give money or goods.

25

c

1. 以下の各種スポーツを表のカテゴリーに従って分類してみましょう。

soccer	swimming	golf
bouldering	skiing	yoga
skydiving	karate	surfing

	Safe	Dangerous
Low cost		
High cost		

2. 1で分類したスポーツから1つを選び、以下の例を参考に英文を完成させ、英語で発表してみましょう。

e.g.
- I chose golf as my topic because I like playing it and watching it.
- I think golf is a safe sport and good exercise.
- However, it costs a lot, especially in Japan, so many young people are not interested in it.

I chose _____ as my topic because _____
_____.

I think _____
_____.

(However, / In addition,) _____
_____.

UNIT 5

Can Fish Fall from the Sky?!

報告する（時事ニュース）

このユニットでは、珍しい気象現象に関する記事を通して、時事ニュースの文体に慣れ、出来事を報告する方法を学びます。

🍪 Pre-reading tasks

A 自分の意見に合うものを［ ］から選ぶか（ ）に記入して、質問に答えましょう。

Q1. Do you check the weather forecast every day?　▶ [Yes. / No.]

Q2. What unusual weather have you experienced?
　　▶ I have experienced [**heavy rain** / **heavy snow** / **a hurricane** /
　　　　（　　　　　　　　）].

B Aの Q1～2 について、クラスメイトの意見を聞いてみましょう。

	Peer #1 Name: _____	Peer #2 Name: _____
Q1.	☐ Yes. ☐ No.	☐ Yes. ☐ No.
Q2.	☐ heavy rain　☐ heavy snow ☐ a hurricane　☐ (　　　　　　)	☐ heavy rain　☐ heavy snow ☐ a hurricane　☐ (　　　　　　)

27

Reading

次の英文を読みましょう（太字は本 Unit の重要語句です）。

Can Fish Fall from the Sky?!

1 People near the coast in Bayland City got a big **surprise** from an afternoon rainstorm Tuesday. Fish from the nearby ocean were falling from the sky. Rebecca Wilson, a **local** mail carrier said: "It was the strangest thing I've ever seen. Little fish about two inches long were coming down with the rain. I walk outside every day, so I've seen every kind of weather you can imagine. I've seen light rain, big heavy rain drops, snow and bits of ice fall from the sky. But this is the first time in my life that I've seen it rain fish!"

2 Although a "shower of fish" is very unusual, it is not unique, and can be **explained** through science. Bob Tyler, a local weather **expert**, said: "When storm **conditions** are just right, it is possible for a **particular** type of small tornado to **form**. This type of tornado can pull up water from rivers, lakes or the ocean, together with things that are in the water. In some **rare** cases, a small tornado can carry large amounts of sucked-up water and **objects**, then drop them over land."

3 Tyler said that Tuesday was not the first day on which fish have fallen from the sky: "It's rare, but not as rare as you might think. It happens about once every 30 years in some areas near the coast." He **added** that it's not just fish that can be sucked up and dropped from the clouds. Flowers, frogs and other small animals, and even pencils and chewing gum are among the things that have been seen coming down in rainstorms over the years.

Notes

l. 1: Bayland City「ベイランド・シティ」(架空の都市名)　l. 3: mail carrier「郵便配達員」　l. 4: inches「インチ」(長さの単位、1インチ＝約 2.5 cm)　l. 13: sucked-up「吸いあげられた」

UNIT 5 Can Fish Fall from the Sky?!

読み方のコツ

時事ニュースでは、人名や団体名などの固有名詞がよくでてきます。各人物・団体の意見や関係性を整理しながら読むとよいでしょう。

Post-reading tasks

A 本文の内容をもとにして以下の図を完成させましょう。

ベイランド・シティの珍事？！

空から小さな（1.　　　）が降ってきた！

（2.　　　）的に説明が可能

- ある種の竜巻が、河川、湖、または（3.　　　）から水と一緒にいろいろなものを吸いあげる

- 時に、その竜巻は、吸いあげた大量の水とものを運び、地上に降らせることがある

- 海岸付近のある地域では、約（4.　　　）年に一度の周期で発生する気象現象

B 次の各文が本文の内容に合っていれば T、間違っていれば F を（　）に記入しましょう。また、その根拠となった本文中の文に下線を引きましょう。

1. (　) People in Bayland City were surprised by unusual weather.
2. (　) Rebecca Wilson has experienced all kinds of weather, except rainstorms.
3. (　) A special type of tornado can form under the right conditions.
4. (　) A "shower of fish" is very unique and has only happened in Bayland City.
5. (　) Only fish can be sucked up and dropped from the sky.

29

c

1. 次のニュースの音声を聞き、a〜e で (1)〜(5) の空所を埋め、以下の表を完成させましょう。

🎧 DL 20   💿 CD 20

- a. People could navigate a ship.
- b. The State University of Tokyo
- c. The National Research Institution for the Environment
- d. The origin of the navigation system
- e. Fish lived around the island.

News	テーマ：The Ancient Navigation System
Teruo Ito	所属：(1) _____ 主張：(2) _____
Miki Sasaki	所属：(3) _____ 主張：(4) _____ 発見：(5) _____ 　　　　= made of bamboo and shells

2. 以下はニュースの概要です。1 の表を参考にして、空所を埋めましょう。

This is the news about _____ . Teruo Ito, the chief researcher of _____ _____ thought fish lived _____ . But Miki Sasaki believed that _____ over a long distance and she found _____ , which was made of bamboo and shells.

UNIT 6

How to Prepare for a Presentation
手順を説明する

このユニットでは、発表の準備の仕方について書かれた文章を通して、手順を説明する方法を学びます。

🫘 Pre-reading tasks

A 自分の意見に合うものを [ ] から選ぶか ( ) に記入して、質問に答えましょう。

Q1. Are you good at giving presentations?　▶ [**Yes.** / **No.**]

Q2. What is the most important thing to prepare for a presentation?
　　▶ I think that [**choosing a topic** / **thinking about the audience** /
　　preparing slides / (　　　　　　　　　　　)] is the most important
　　thing.

B A の Q1～2 について、クラスメイトの意見を聞いてみましょう。

	Peer #1 Name: _____	Peer #2 Name: _____
Q1.	☐ Yes. ☐ No.	☐ Yes. ☐ No.
Q2.	☐ choosing a topic ☐ thinking about the audience ☐ preparing slides ☐ (　　　　　　　　　)	☐ choosing a topic ☐ thinking about the audience ☐ preparing slides ☐ (　　　　　　　　　)

Reading

次の英文を読みましょう（太字は本 Unit の重要語句です）。

How to Prepare for a Presentation

1 Here's how to get ready for a presentation. First, you need to choose a **topic**, such as a report on a book you have read. Second, you need to understand what the people who will be in your **audience** already know about your topic. An audience of experts will expect a different **presentation** than a general audience would. Next, you have to decide how you want the audience to feel after the presentation is finished. In our example, let's say the book is one that your classmates are not **familiar with**, which makes them a general audience. Also, the purpose of your presentation is to explain why you liked the book.

2 You should plan the **content** of your presentation "**conclusion** first." That is, write your conclusion before you do anything else. Everything in your presentation should **lead to** that conclusion. In other words, everything you mention in your presentation should be about the book or why you think it is good.

3 After you create the conclusion it is time to write your **introduction**, which is really another version of the conclusion. Do you think it will be boring for your audience to discover that your introduction and conclusion are similar? Don't worry! Remember, the book is new to your audience. They need to understand what you are going to tell them, and repeating your main points helps the audience follow your presentation.

4 Finally, it is time to explain each of the reasons why you liked the book. **Be sure to** keep these explanations in the same order they appear in the introduction and conclusion. As a result your presentation will be very clear because you will, in your introduction, tell your audience what you will tell them. Next, in the body of your presentation, you will tell them what you **promised** to tell them. Finally, in the conclusion, you will tell them what you told them. It's that easy!

Notes

l. 6: let's say 「たとえば」　l. 14: it is time to 「〜する番です、〜するときです」

UNIT 6 How to Prepare for a Presentation

読み方のコツ

手順を説明する文章を読む際には、first、second、または next などの語が、手順のみならず文章構造を理解するのに役に立ちます。

Post-reading tasks

A 本文の内容をもとにして以下の図を完成させましょう。

わかりやすい発表の準備の仕方

Step 1
a. (1.   ) を選択する
b. (2.   ) がすでに知っていることを分析する
c. 発表で何を伝えたいのかを決める

【例】 a. 自分が読んだ本について
b. (2.   ) は本についてなじみがない
c. なぜその本が好きなのかを説明する

Step 2 最初に結論から書く

Step 3 (3.   ) を書く

Step 4 最後に (4.   ) を書く

B 次の各文が本文の内容に合っていれば T、間違っていれば F を (　　) に記入しましょう。また、その根拠となった本文中の文に下線を引きましょう。

1. (　) Before you do anything else, you should decide what you are going to talk about.
2. (　) If you choose a book that your classmates are familiar with, you can make them a general audience.
3. (　) Every piece of information provided in your presentation should be linked to the conclusion.
4. (　) There is no relationship between the introduction and conclusion.
5. (　) Repeating the main points in the conclusion helps the audience better understand your presentation.

c

1. 以下はパーティーを準備するための手順です。音声を聞いて、正しい順番になるように番号を記入しましょう。最初の手順には 1 がすでに記入されています。

   🎧 DL 25　💿 CD 25

   (　　) **a.** Plan the guest list.
   (　　) **b.** Decide food and drinks.
   (　　) **c.** Welcome the guests with music.
   (　　) **d.** Send e-mails to the guests.
   (1) **e.** Decide an appropriate date, time, and place.

2. パーティーをよりよいものにするために、上記 a ～ e の他に新たに 2 つの手順を加え、以下のリストを完成させましょう。なお、新たな手順を加える位置は、どこでもかまいません。

How to Plan a Party	
1	Decide an appropriate date, time, and place.

3. 以下の例を参考にしながら、2 で作成したリストをペアになって発表してみましょう。

   e.g.
   First, decide an appropriate date, time, and place. **Second**, decide the theme of the party and dress code. **Next**, plan the guest list …. **Finally**, ….

UNIT 7

International Date Line

事実を時系列に沿って説明する

このユニットでは、自国の標準時を何度も変更したサモアについて書かれた文章を通して、事実関係を時系列に沿って説明する方法を学びます。

🏉 Pre-reading tasks

A 自分の意見に合うものを［ ］から選ぶか（ ）に記入して、質問に答えましょう。

Q1. Have you visited any South Pacific islands?　▶ [Yes. / No.]

Q2. What image do you have of Samoa?
　　▶ I think Samoa is a [**tropical** / **friendly** / **beautiful** / (　　　　　　)] country.

B AのQ1〜2について、クラスメイトの意見を聞いてみましょう。

	Peer #1 Name: _____	Peer #2 Name: _____
Q1.	☐ Yes.　☐ No. → If yes, which islands? (　　　　　　　　　　)	☐ Yes.　☐ No. → If yes, which islands? (　　　　　　　　　　)
Q2.	☐ tropical　☐ friendly ☐ beautiful　☐ (　　　　　)	☐ tropical　☐ friendly ☐ beautiful　☐ (　　　　　)

Reading

次の英文を読みましょう（太字は本 Unit の重要語句です）。

International Date Line

1 Life is short, but it's even shorter when your country loses a day. Such was the **case** when the tiny South Pacific island nation of Samoa moved from the east to the west side of the International Date Line. On Thursday, December 29th, 2011 when the clock struck midnight the country moved 24 hours ahead straight to Saturday, December 31st. However, this was not the first time Samoa made such a **switch**.

2 Before 1892 Samoa lay to the west of the line, but U.S. business people **persuaded** Samoans to match their time with nearby U.S. controlled American Samoa and the U.S. Pacific Coast to make trading easier. Before the change, business orders made from Samoa Monday were not **processed** until Tuesday, which was actually Monday, U.S. time. The change made international trade between Samoa and North America much more **convenient** and indicated North America's power and **authority** in the Pacific **region**.

3 However, times change. One hundred nineteen years later in June 2011, the Samoan government passed a law moving Samoa back to the west of the date line to ease trade with its modern-day business partners in the West Pacific. Now, when it's Monday in Samoa, it's also Monday for key trade partners like New Zealand, Australia, and East Asian countries such as China. This time shift, as well as new traffic rules which match many of these important trading partners, clearly shows the change of **influence** in the Pacific region.

4 There is little **doubt** that the time change was beneficial to Samoa's economic future, but what about the lost day? The Samoan government ruled that those scheduled to work on the missing Friday be fully paid for the lost day of **labor**. However, Samoans have to decide whether those born on December 30th actually aged on that missing day.

Notes

l. 8: American Samoa「アメリカ領サモア」（1899 年にアメリカ領となる）　l. 16: modern-day「今日の、現代の」　l. 21: beneficial「有益な」

UNIT 7　International Date Line

> **読み方のコツ**
>
> 時系列に沿って情報が書かれている文章では、年号や日時をおさえながら整理して読むとよいでしょう。それぞれの年号や日時に、どこで、どんな出来事がおこったのかを図にして簡潔に示すと、全体像が理解しやすくなるでしょう。

Post-reading tasks

A 本文の内容をもとにして以下の表を完成させましょう。

変更時期	(1.　　　)年	2011年
サモアの位置移動	国際日付変更線の西側 →(2.　　　)側へ	国際日付変更線の東側 →西側へ
移動の理由	貿易をしやすくするため	貿易をしやすくするため
主な貿易相手国	北アメリカの国々	ニュージーランド (3.　　　　　　) 東アジアの国々

B 次の各文が本文の内容に合っていればT、間違っていればFを（　）に記入しましょう。また、その根拠となった本文中の文に下線を引きましょう。

1. (　) The tiny island of Samoa actually moved to the West Pacific by being pushed by waves.
2. (　) The change in 2011 was the first time for Samoa to make a switch to another side of the International Date Line.
3. (　) The Samoan government passed a law moving Samoa back to the west of the date line.
4. (　) Today, Samoa's business partners are different from those in 1892.
5. (　) People in Samoa enjoy economic benefits of the time change.

1. 自分自身について振り返り、例を参考に以下の表を完成させましょう。

e.g.

Year	Events	Name of place, school, or company	Notes
2000	born	Takarazuka, Hyogo	the oldest child in my family
2006	entered school	Takarazuka Elementary School	made good friends

Year	Events	Name of place, school, or company	Notes

2. 1でまとめた内容と以下の例を参考に、簡単な自伝をノートに書いてみましょう。

e.g.

I was born in 2000 in Takarazuka, Hyogo. I'm the oldest child in my family. I went to Takarazuka Elementary School when I was six. I don't remember much, but I made a lot of good friends ....

UNIT 8

What Is Friendship?

定義を示して例示する

このユニットでは、友情について書かれた文章を通して、抽象的な話題を、定義と具体例を示して説明する方法を学びます。

🍵 Pre-reading tasks

A 自分の意見に合うものを [ ] から選ぶか ( ) に記入して、質問に答えましょう。

Q1. Do you think that friendship is important in your life?　▶ [**Yes.** / **No.**]

Q2. What do you think is important for keeping a good friendship?
　▶ I think that being [**kind** / **honest** / **supportive** / (　　　　　)] is important for keeping a good friendship.

B A の Q1～2 について、クラスメイトの意見を聞いてみましょう。

	Peer #1 Name: _____	Peer #2 Name: _____
Q1.	☐ Yes. ☐ No.	☐ Yes. ☐ No.
Q2.	☐ kind　☐ honest　☐ supportive ☐ (　　　　　　　)	☐ kind　☐ honest　☐ supportive ☐ (　　　　　　　)

What Is Friendship?

1 Friendship is a very important part of our lives. Our friends are like a second family that supports us when we need help. Without them, life would be more difficult and we would be poorer as individuals. Therefore, we must think about the meaning of this kind of relationship.

2 People do not usually **share** their thoughts and feelings with **strangers**, but they do with friends. This is one reason why friendship is special. It means there is someone you can **communicate with** and who understands you. You can speak openly and never worry about being judged by that person. He or she knows all about you; your good points and your bad points, and **accepts** both.

3 Being honest is also part of a relationship between friends. This means you do not always have to agree with a friend's opinion. Nor do you stay silent when, in fact, you want to disagree with him or her. When you think your friend is in the wrong, you tell him or her directly. As well as being honest, you greatly **value** your friend's **opinions**—even when they are different from your own.

4 Friendship does not only **exist** between humans. Many people have pets that they consider friends. Of course owners and animals cannot communicate through words, but they often communicate through feelings and actions. The best example is a dog. If it is **treated** well, it is devoted to its owner. It understands **warmth** and kindness and will protect the owner. In this case, the owner usually feels like a friend of the dog, not its owner, and is devoted to the animal.

5 **Maintaining** friendships can sometimes be difficult, but friends make our lives richer. Because of them, we are able to speak from the heart and become more understanding as well as more caring individuals.

Notes

l. 3: therefore「したがって、それゆえに」　l. 18: be devoted to「〜に（努力や愛情などを）ささげる、専念する」

UNIT 8　What Is Friendship?

読み方のコツ

抽象的な概念を説明する際には、定義だけではなく、like「〜のような」や The best example is「最たる例は〜です」といった表現を使い、具体例が示されることがあるので注意しましょう。

Post-reading tasks

A 本文の内容をもとにして以下の図を完成させましょう。

```
( 1.          )  ＝  とても大切なもの
```

友達とは…

- 自分の（2.　　　）や気持ちを話せる人
- 自分を（3.　　　）してくれる人

友達に対して…

（4.　　　）であるべき

B 次の各文が本文の内容に合っていれば T、間違っていれば F を（　）に記入しましょう。また、その根拠となった本文中の文に下線を引きましょう。

1. (　) People do not usually open their hearts to strangers.
2. (　) You ignore your friends' opinions when they are different from yours.
3. (　) Pet owners and their pets cannot understand each other through feelings and actions.
4. (　) If you treat your dog well, it will be devoted to you.
5. (　) It is sometimes difficult to keep a good relationship with our friends.

c

1. 以下のa～dから2つを選び、英英辞書の定義を書き、独自の定義を考えてみましょう。

> **a.** failure　　**b.** happiness　　**c.** freedom　　**d.** respect

Word: (　　　　　　　　　　)

English-English dictionary	
Your definition	

Word: (　　　　　　　　　　)

English-English dictionary	
Your definition	

2. クラスメイトにインタビューをして、様々な独自の定義を集めてみましょう。

e.g. What did you choose?
　　　What does ＿＿＿＿＿＿＿ mean to you?

Peer #1　Name: ＿＿＿＿＿＿＿＿＿＿＿＿

Word	Definition

Peer #2　Name: ＿＿＿＿＿＿＿＿＿＿＿＿

Word	Definition

Peer #3　Name: ＿＿＿＿＿＿＿＿＿＿＿＿

Word	Definition

UNIT 9

Entering a Photo Contest

効率的に情報を伝える（e-mail）

このユニットでは、2通の e-mail を通して、効率的に情報を伝える方法や、英文 e-mail の書き方を学びます。

Pre-reading tasks

A 自分の意見に合うものを ［ ］ から選ぶか （ ） に記入して、質問に答えましょう。

Q1. Have you ever written e-mails in English?　▶ [**Yes.** / **No.**]

Q2. What do you think is important when writing e-mails?
　▶ I think that [**grammar** / **accuracy** / **politeness** / (　　　　　)]
　　is important when writing e-mails.

B Ⓐ の Q1〜2 について、クラスメイトの意見を聞いてみましょう。

	Peer #1 Name: _____	Peer #2 Name: _____
Q1.	☐ Yes. ☐ No.	☐ Yes. ☐ No.
Q2.	☐ grammar　☐ accuracy ☐ politeness　☐ (　　　　　)	☐ grammar　☐ accuracy ☐ politeness　☐ (　　　　　)

Reading

次の英文を読みましょう（太字は本 Unit の重要語句です）。

Entering a Photo Contest

E-mail 1

1 *A photographer writes an e-mail asking about a photo contest's rules.*

To: Rick Lee
From: Amy Paulson
Subject: Photo contest rules

Hello Mr. Lee,

My name is Amy Paulson and I am writing about the 15th **Annual** Photo Contest for Beginners. I have a few questions about the rules of the **competition**.

2 First of all, I am not a **professional** photographer, but I have been paid for taking pictures at a few weddings. I would like to know if I can still enter the contest even though I'm not a total beginner.

3 Second, I would like to know a little more about acceptable content for the photographs. I understand that this year's **theme** is nature, but I would like to know if people or animals can also **appear** in the images.

I am looking forward to hearing from you soon.

Thank you very much,
Amy Paulson

E-mail 2

4 *A judge writes back to a photographer about the contest rules.*

To: Amy Paulson
From: Rick Lee
Subject: Re: Photo contest rules

Hello Ms. Paulson,

Thank you very much for your interest in entering our competition. We are always very happy to answer **contestants**' questions.

5 You are right that the contest is not open to **career** photographers. However, since you have only been paid a few times and you are not really a professional, you can enter the contest. Most of our contestants have some **previous** experience with photography.

6 On the other hand, I'm sorry to say that contest rules clearly **state** that only photographs of nature will be accepted. Photos of wild animals like rabbits or birds are okay, but people and pets such as cats and dogs should not appear in the images.

I hope that **clears up** your concerns about the contest. Please keep the closing date of January 21st in mind. We are looking forward to seeing your photographs.

Sincerely,
Rick Lee

Notes
l. 12: acceptable「受理可能な」 l. 36: sincerely「敬具」（e-mail や手紙の結辞）

読み方のコツ
e-mail では、相手に情報を効率的に伝えるために、冒頭で用件を簡潔に述べ、その後、内容の詳細を述べることが多いようです。このような文章構成を念頭に、e-mail を読むとよいでしょう。

Post-reading tasks

A 本文の内容をもとにして以下の表を完成させましょう。

	E-mail 1	E-mail 2
差出人	Amy Paulson	(1.)
用件	コンテストの(2.)に関する問合せ	問合せへの回答
内容	問合せ・回答1：コンテストに(3.)できるかどうかについて 問合せ・回答2：コンテストに応募できる写真の(4.)について	

B 次の各文が本文の内容に合っていればT、間違っていればFを（　）に記入しましょう。また、その根拠となった本文中の文に下線を引きましょう。

1. (　) The photo competition for beginners is held every year.
2. (　) Ms. Paulson took photographs at some weddings and was paid for them.
3. (　) Mr. Lee is interested in entering the photo competition.
4. (　) Ms. Paulson is not able to enter the photo contest due to her past experience.
5. (　) January 1st is the deadline for entering the contest.

C 以下は、授業を欠席することになり、宿題について先生に問い合わせる e-mail です。空所を埋めて、e-mail を完成させましょう。

Subject: _____

Dear _____,

I am writing about _____. Unfortunately, I am not able to attend _____ because of _____. Could you please _____?
I appreciate your understanding in this matter.

Kind regards,

_____

UNIT 10

Getting Money for a Big Project

比較する

このユニットでは、資金を集める2つの方法について比較した文章を通して、類似点や相違点を説明する方法を学びます。

🌱 Pre-reading tasks

A 自分の意見に合うものを [ ] から選ぶか（ ）に記入して、質問に答えましょう。

Q1. Would you like to have your own business?　▶ [Yes. / No.]

Q2. What do you think is important to make business run smoothly?
　　▶ I think that [**money** / **human resources** / **connections** /
　　（　　　　　　　　　　）] is/are important.

B A の Q1〜2 について、クラスメイトの意見を聞いてみましょう。

	Peer #1 Name: _____	Peer #2 Name: _____
Q1.	☐ Yes.　☐ No. → If yes, what kind? (　　　　　　　　　　　)	☐ Yes.　☐ No. → If yes, what kind? (　　　　　　　　　　　)
Q2.	☐ money　☐ human resources ☐ connections ☐ (　　　　　　　　　　)	☐ money　☐ human resources ☐ connections ☐ (　　　　　　　　　　)

Reading

次の英文を読みましょう（太字は本 Unit の重要語句です）。

Getting Money for a Big Project

1 There are two ways to **borrow** large amounts of money: go to a bank for a loan, or get money from a group of individuals.

2 It is very **common** for a business to get a loan from a bank. The bank is asked to **provide** some money, and the bank decides how much money to give, and how it will be paid back. After the loan is made, the business uses the money to start a new project or continue to **operate** during a slow business period. The business then **prepares** to pay back the original loan amount, known as the principal, and the interest, which is the bank's charge for using its money.

3 Instead of borrowing money from a bank, a business can borrow a large amount of money from individuals by selling bonds. A bond is a piece of paper that **describes** a loan **contract** between a business or government and the lender of the money. Thus, if you buy a bond, then you are lending money to a business just like a bank would. In addition, the business will pay your money back, with interest, just like it would pay back a bank that loaned it money.

4 A big difference between a bank loan and a bond is the number of people **involved**. Bank loans usually involve one bank and one loan. On the other hand, companies or governments can sell thousands or millions of bonds to individuals or businesses. Using bonds, they can raise the huge amounts of money needed for big projects. Asking a single bank for such large sums of money would only **result in** the answer "No, we don't have that much money to lend." But if many individuals lend a company or a government a somewhat small amount of money each, then the total amount borrowed can become **extremely** large.

Notes

l. 6: slow business period「経営不振期」　l. 8: principal「元金」（貸し借りしたもとの金）
l. 8: interest「利子」　l. 10: bonds「債券」（会社などが資金を借り入れる際に発行する社債などの有価証券）
l. 12: lender「貸手、金貸し」　l. 19: sums「金額」（large sums of money「多額のお金」）
l. 21: somewhat「いくらか、多少」

UNIT 10 Getting Money for a Big Project

読み方のコツ

比較の文章では、2つ（以上）の事柄を比べ、類似点や相違点を示すために、A is similar to B in ~「AとBは~の点で似ています」や、A (big) difference between A and B is ~「AとBの（大きな）違いは~です」といった表現が使われます。

Post-reading tasks

A 本文の内容をもとにして以下の表を完成させましょう。

お金を借りる方法	ローンを組む	(1.　　　　)を売却(発行)する
借入先	(2.　　　　)	個人グループ
借入金の(3.　　　　)方法	もとの借入額に(4.　　　　)をつけて(3.　　　　)する	
借り入れできる総額	ある程度限られている	巨額の資金を借り得る

B 次の各文が本文の内容に合っていればT、間違っていればFを（　）に記入しましょう。また、その根拠となった本文中の文に下線を引きましょう。

1. (　) It is quite usual for a business to borrow money from a bank.
2. (　) The principal is the bank's charge for using its money.
3. (　) Buying a bond means borrowing money from the business.
4. (　) Bank loans usually involve a smaller number of people than selling bonds.
5. (　) It is not difficult to get extremely large amounts of money from a bank.

49

C

1. 例を参考に比較する題材を考え、類似点と相違点を2つ以上あげて以下の図に記入しましょう。

   e.g.

   Soccer   **Baseball**

Soccer	共通	Baseball
11 players	use balls	9 players
use feet	popular sports	use gloves
90 minutes	professional leagues	9 innings

   [　　　　　　　]   [　　　　　　　]

2. 上記の1の内容と以下の例を参考に、類似点と相違点を含む英文をノートに書き、ペアになって発表してみましょう。類似点と相違点の表現集も参考にしてみましょう。

   e.g.
   - Soccer and baseball **both** use balls.
   - **Like** soccer, baseball is a very popular sport among young people.
   - **However**, there are many **differences** between the two sports.
   - There are usually 11 players on a soccer team. **On the other hand**, there are only 9 players on a baseball team.
   - **Unlike** baseball, soccer players do not use any tools such as gloves and bats.

〈表現集〉

類似点	相違点
both / like / same / similar to / in the same way	different / on the other hand / unlike / in contrast to / instead of

UNIT 11

Accepting the "Salesperson of the Year" Award

スピーチの文体に慣れる

このユニットでは、年間優秀販売員のスピーチ原稿を通して、スピーチの文体と方法について学びます。

🍵 Pre-reading tasks

A 自分の意見に合うものを [ ] から選ぶか ( ) に記入して、質問に答えましょう。

Q1. Have you ever given a speech? ▶ [**Yes.** / **No.**]

Q2. What do you check before you buy a product?
▶ Before I buy a product, I check [**websites** / **friends' comments** / **magazines** / (　　　　　　　)].

B AのQ1～2について、クラスメイトの意見を聞いてみましょう。

	Peer #1 Name: _____	Peer #2 Name: _____
Q1.	☐ Yes. ☐ No. → If yes, what about? (　　　　　　　　　)	☐ Yes. ☐ No. → If yes, what about? (　　　　　　　　　)
Q2.	☐ websites ☐ friends' comments ☐ magazines ☐ (　　　　　　　)	☐ websites ☐ friends' comments ☐ magazines ☐ (　　　　　　　)

Reading

次の英文を読みましょう（太字は本 Unit の重要語句です）。

Accepting the "Salesperson of the Year" Award

1 Thank you all so much for this great **honor**. A year ago, I could never have dreamed that I would be named "Salesperson of the Year." The economy was weak, our **product** was unknown, and the company was not making any money. I thought all of us would be looking for new jobs very soon. But we turned it around! Our product is now number one in the **market**, and the company is stronger than ever. I wish I could take credit for this, but in truth the credit belongs to all of you. It was a group **effort**. In accepting this award, I would like to thank the advertising team and the support staff.

2 First, I want to thank the advertising team. Without their great work, our sales would not have **improved**. A year ago, we knew we had a great product, but no one else did. The advertising team studied the market, **figured out** who would want to buy our product, and found a way to reach them. Without their great work, our product would still be **unknown** today.

3 Second, I want to thank the support staff for taking such good care of our **customers**. Our product is not easy to use, and customers had many questions after purchase. But our support staff was up to the challenge. On call twenty-four hours a day, they listened to our customers carefully and answered their questions clearly and **politely**. Because of the excellent support, our customers spoke well of our product to others, and our sales grew as a result.

4 No salesperson **succeeds** without a strong team. I am very lucky to have such a wonderful group of people supporting me, and I am truly grateful for your efforts this past year. Let's make next year even better! Thank you all very much.

Notes

l. 2: Salesperson of the Year「年間優秀販売員」 l. 4: turn it around「好転させる」
l. 6: take credit for「〜を自分の手柄にする」 l. 16: up to the challenge「挑戦を受けて立つ」
l. 19: speak well of「〜についてよく話す」 l. 21: grateful for「〜に感謝する」

UNIT 11 Accepting the "Salesperson of the Year" Award

読み方のコツ

スピーチでは、比較的平易な文体が使われ、また、最初に謝辞が述べられてから具体的なエピソードに展開することが多くあります。こうした文体と構成を理解し、話者の思いに気持ちを重ねながら読んでみましょう。

Post-reading tasks

A 本文の内容をもとにして以下の図を完成させましょう。

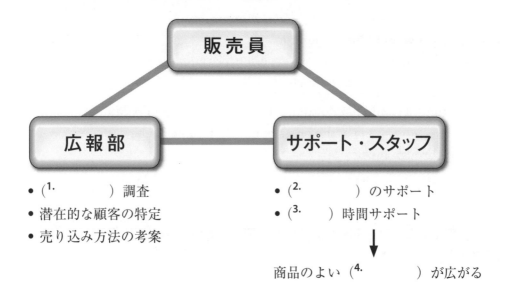

年間優秀販売員を支えたチーム力

販売員

広報部
- (1.　　　) 調査
- 潜在的な顧客の特定
- 売り込み方法の考案

サポート・スタッフ
- (2.　　　) のサポート
- (3.　) 時間サポート

↓

商品のよい (4.　　　) が広がる

B 次の各文が本文の内容に合っていればT、間違っていればFを（　）に記入しましょう。また、その根拠となった本文中の文に下線を引きましょう。

1. (　) The speaker has been dreaming of being "Salesperson of the Year" for long time.

2. (　) A year ago, even though the economy was weak, the product was selling well.

3. (　) The advertising team found potential customers and a way to approach them.

4. (　) The product is user-friendly and customers are able to use it without any problem.

5. (　) According to the speaker, providing great support to the customers eventually resulted in sales growth.

C

1. あるスピーチの冒頭部分の音声を聞き、以下の表を英語または日本語で完成させましょう。

🎧 DL 49　💿 CD 49

誰に向けたスピーチですか？	(1)
話者が受賞したのは？	(2)
何の式典でのスピーチですか？	(3)

2. 以下は、1 のスピーチの続きです。音声を聞き、空所を適語で埋めましょう。

🎧 DL 50　💿 CD 50

First, **I would like to thank** my (1.　　　　　). Because of them, I got to travel to many places. Those experiences taught me that there is a lot more to (2.　　　　　) than just textbooks.

Second, I would like to thank my teachers, especially Mr. Jackson. He was the (3.　　　　　) of the brass band. **He taught me** how to (4.　　　　　) myself through music.

Thirdly, I would like to thank my friends. **Without their support, I** would not have been able to (5.　　　　　) my goals.

We are leaving this school today. The future is truly within our hands. Thank you.

3. 2 のスクリプトを参考に、誰かに感謝の意を伝える英文を完成させ、英語で発表してみましょう。英文を変えたり、追加したりしてもかまいません。

Tips for the task

- I would like to thank _____ . ［感謝の意を伝える相手］

- He/She/They (taught / helped / showed / ...) me _____ .
  　　　　　　　　　　　　　　　　　　　　　　　　　［相手がしてくれたこと］

- Without his/her/their support, I _____ .
  　　　　　　　　　　　　　　　　［相手のサポートがなかったらどうなっていたか］

UNIT 12

Written Art

コミュニケーションのスタイルを理解する

このユニットでは、手書きの文字とインターネットで使われる顔文字などに関する文章を通して、コミュニケーションスタイルについて学びます。

Pre-reading tasks

A 1〜5はインターネットでよく使われる省略記号・文字です。対応するメッセージをa〜eから1つ選び、それぞれを線で結びましょう。

1. :~)
2. g/f
3. EM
4. IYO
5. :c

a. in your opinion
b. cute
c. sad
d. girlfriend
e. e-mail

B 以下の省略文字がどのようなメッセージを意味しているのか考えてみましょう。その後で、クラスメイトと答え合わせをしてみましょう。

1. OTOH _____
2. F2F _____
3. PLZ _____
4. TTUS _____

Reading

次の英文を読みましょう（太字は本 Unit の重要語句です）。

Written Art

1 When most people write these days, they do not use pens or pencils. Instead, they press buttons or touch **screens**. Because of this, the **beauty** of handwriting itself is being lost. Speed is more important.

2 However, messages written with a pen or pencil often **reveal** the character of writers. They show how much thought **went into** creating the content. Also, the beautiful strokes that link each letter reveal the writer's sense of art. Do you think the **following** letter is like art?

Hello Mark,

I met Karen, today. She is so cute! I wish she were my girlfriend. I want to tell her that, and I am thinking of sending her an e-mail. In your opinion, is it a good idea? On the other hand, maybe I should tell her face-to-face. Please help me decide! I am worried and will feel really sad if she is not interested in me.

Talk to you soon,

Ken

3 Maybe your answer is "Yes" and perhaps it's "No," but **social** networking sites such as Twitter and Facebook are changing the way we write—and some people do not like the change. They say the **messages** mostly **contain** simple English, so the language is losing its good qualities. But these messages often contain **symbols** and letters instead of words, which bring an **element** of interest and art. For example, the following letter contains the same information as the previous one:

Mark,

I met Karen, today. She's so :~)! I wish she were my g/f. I want to tell her that, and I'm thinking of sending her an EM. IYO, is it a good idea? OTOH, maybe I should tell her F2F. PLZ help me decide! I'm worried and will feel really :c if she's not interested in me. TTUS,

Ken

In your opinion, which letter is more like "art"?

> **Notes**
> l. 2: handwriting「手書き」　l. 6: strokes「筆跡」

> **読み方のコツ**
> 単語や文字などのスタイルの違いは、「何の目的で」、「誰を対象にして」、「どのような調子で」、文章が書かれたかを反映しています。スタイルに隠された書き手の意図にも注意するとよいでしょう。

Post-reading tasks

A 本文の内容をもとにして以下の図を完成させましょう。

どちらがより芸術的？

手書きの文字表現

ペンや鉛筆の筆跡は、書き手の（1. 　　　　　）や芸術的な感性を表す
近年、（2. 　　　　　）がより重要になり、手書きの価値が軽視されつつある

新しい文字表現

TwitterやFacebookなどの（3. 　　　　　　　　　）が誕生
ネット上では、簡単な英語、特殊な（4. 　　　　　）や文字が使われている

B 次の各文が本文の内容に合っていればT、間違っていればFを（　）に記入しましょう。また、その根拠となった本文中の文に下線を引きましょう。

1. (　) Most people still prefer to use pens or pencils instead of computers or smartphones.
2. (　) People emphasize the importance of speed in writing.
3. (　) We are able to understand the personality of writers through looking at their handwriting.
4. (　) Recent online services have an effect on our way of writing.
5. (　) The second letter contains less information than the first one.

C

1. (1)〜(4)はインターネットでよく使われる省略文字です。対応するメッセージをa〜dから1つ選び、それぞれを線で結びましょう。

    (1) 2moro　•　　　•　a. please tell me
    (2) HV　　•　　　•　b. wait
    (3) W8　　•　　　•　c. tomorrow
    (4) PTM　•　　　•　d. have

2. 1と本文で学習した省略文字を使って、以下の手紙をe-mailにしてノートに書き直してみましょう。

Dear Kenji,

Thank you for your e-mail. It's very kind of you to share your ideas. In your opinion, should we wait for a while until the final decision is made? I would like to have a face-to-face meeting tomorrow. Please tell me if you are available.

Talk to you soon,

Aki

UNIT 13

Life Advice Q & A with Dr. Joyce Green

目的をもって尋ねる（人生相談）

このユニットでは、ストレスに関するQ & A形式の文章を通して、目的をもって尋ねる方法を学びます。

Pre-reading tasks

A 自分の意見に合うものを [ ] から選ぶか（ ）に記入して、質問に答えましょう。

Q1. Do you feel a lot of stress? ▶ [**Yes.** / **No.**]

Q2. What do you do when you feel stress?
  ▶ When I feel stress, I like to [**read books** / **sleep** / **go shopping** /
  (   )].

B AのQ1〜2について、クラスメイトの意見を聞いてみましょう。

	Peer #1 Name: _____	Peer #2 Name: _____
Q1.	☐ Yes. ☐ No.	☐ Yes. ☐ No.
Q2.	☐ read books ☐ sleep ☐ go shopping ☐ ( )	☐ read books ☐ sleep ☐ go shopping ☐ ( )

Reading

次の英文を読みましょう（太字は本 Unit の重要語句です）。

Life Advice Q & A with Dr. Joyce Green

1 Many readers have written me to ask about how to **handle** stress. Here are some typical questions from readers, and my answers.

Q: How much stress is too much?

A: Stress can't be **measured** or counted easily, like money or food. But if you think about it carefully, you will develop a sense of how strongly it **affects** you, and how to handle it.

2 Q: What kinds of stress are there?

A: I usually think of different kinds of stress as coming from different sources. For example, I have family-related stress, stress from work, stress from worrying about my weight and **appearance**, physical stress from exercise, and physical stress from working at a computer all day.

3 Q: How can we tell good stress from bad stress?

A: I think that any kind of stress can be good or bad. The important thing is getting the right **amount** of stress. In my own life, family-related stress is usually good. Caring for my children and husband is a big challenge. But I can handle it. It gives me stress, but also a lot of satisfaction.

4 Q: What can we do about stress from work?

A: Stress from work can also be **satisfying**. The right amount of it helps us learn new things, earn more money, and find ways to help others. But work often gives us too much stress. How do you know when you have too much stress at work? In my case, my hands hurt from typing too much, and my **stomach** sometimes hurts also. Can you **identify** the signs of unhealthy stress in your life? This is an important step toward **managing** your stress. When you understand which type of stress you get too much of, the next step is finding ways to reduce it. That's what we'll **cover** next week.

Notes

l. 9: family-related「家族関連の」　l. 16: satisfaction「満足感」

UNIT 13 Life Advice Q & A with Dr. Joyce Green

> **読み方のコツ**
>
> Q＆A形式の文章では、質問（Q）を先に読むことで、文章全体のイメージをつかむことができます。また、答え（A）の中で、重要と思える箇所に下線を引いておくと、内容の振り返りがしやすくなります。

Post-reading tasks

A 本文の内容をもとにして以下の表を完成させましょう。

読者からの質問	ジョイス・グリーン博士の回答
ストレスの量について	ストレスは簡単に（1.　　　　　　）ない。しかし真剣に考えれば、ストレスへの対応の感覚を磨くことができる
ストレスの種類について	ストレスは原因が違えば、（2.　　　　　　）も異なる
良いストレスと悪いストレスの見分け方	すべてのストレスは良くも悪くもなる。大切なのは（3.　　　　　　）のストレスを受けること
仕事によるストレスについて	適度なストレスは以下3つの助けとなる： 1. 新しい物事を学ぶこと 2. （4.　　　　　　　　　　） 3. 他者を助ける方法を見つけること

B 次の各文が本文の内容に合っていればT、間違っていればFを（　）に記入しましょう。また、その根拠となった本文中の文に下線を引きましょう。

1. (　) Many readers have written to Dr. Green to ask about how to handle family problems.
2. (　) Dr. Green doesn't have any physical stress.
3. (　) For Dr. Green, caring for her family provides her with a lot of satisfaction.
4. (　) In the case of Dr. Green, a stomachache is one sign of too much stress.
5. (　) Dr. Green will give readers ways to relieve stomach pain next week.

C

1. やることが多く、とても忙しい時、どのように対処していますか。本文や以下の例を参考にしながら、質問に対して自分の答えを書いてみましょう。

   Q1. What do you use for scheduling?
   e.g. I use a(n) (notebook / online system / application / …) for scheduling.

   _____

   Q2. How do you deal with stress caused by a busy schedule?
   e.g. I listen to relaxing music. / I call my friends.

   _____

2. 1のQ1とQ2についてクラスメイトにインタビューして、様々な意見を集めてみましょう。

   Peer #1   Name: _____

Q1.	
Q2.	

   Peer #2   Name: _____

Q1.	
Q2.	

   Peer #3   Name: _____

Q1.	
Q2.	

UNIT 14

The Economy Is Strong, for Now

経済記事を読んでグラフを完成させる

このユニットでは、日本経済に関する記事を通して、データを使いながら事実を説明したり、グラフで表す方法を学びます。

🫘 Pre-reading tasks

A 1〜5は経済に関する単語・表現です。対応する意味をa〜eから1つ選び、それぞれを線で結びましょう。

1. unemployment rate
2. recession
3. stock market
4. long-term economic growth
5. minimum wages

a. 株式市場
b. 長期経済成長
c. 最低賃金
d. 不況
e. 失業率

B 以下の単語について調べ、どのような現象を指すのか日本語でまとめてみましょう。その後で、クラスメイトと答え合わせをしてみましょう。

1. Inflation	2. Deflation

The Economy Is Strong, for Now

By Takeshi Suzuki, June 25, 2020

1 An economist has described the Japanese **economy** as very strong. She **notes** several strengths to support her conclusion. She also notes one long-term concern.

2 Mitsuko Kato, professor of economics at the National Institute of Economics, writes a daily blog called *Economic Times*. In it, she discusses Japan's economic future. Many business leaders look to her for ideas about the economy. Yesterday, she **issued** her annual statement on the strength of the economy.

3 On the positive side, Kato writes that **wages** are increasing. In 2015, the average worker's wages increased only 0.5 percent for the year. Last year, however, wages grew 2.0 percent. Kato thinks that they will increase 3.5 percent this year. Also, fewer people are looking for work. The **unemployment** rate was 5.3 percent in 2015. Last year, it dropped to 4.2 percent. Kato sees this **figure** dropping to 3.8 percent this year. She also points to an improved **stock market**. A leading stock market index stood at 13,500 points ten years ago. In 2015, it had dropped to 12,000. Today, it stands at 16,000. Kato **expects** it to rise to 21,000 by the end of 2021. These are signs of a strong economy, indeed.

4 But Kato also issued a warning about inflation. Inflation is the increase in the cost of goods and services. Economists are generally happy if inflation **remains** under 2.0 percent each year. If the economy heats up too quickly, and demand for goods and services increases, it might lead to a sharp rise in inflation. Kato points out that inflation was steady from 2015 to 2017, averaging 0.5 percent per year. However, inflation was 1.5 percent in 2018 and 2.5 percent in 2019. Kato fears that it could rise above 3.0 percent next year. That could put the economy **at risk**.

Notes

l. 7: look to「〜を当てにする、〜に頼る」 l. 8: annual statement「年間報告書」 l. 8: the strength of the economy「経済力」 l. 14: point to「〜を指摘する」 l. 15: stand at「〜に達する」

UNIT 14 The Economy Is Strong, for Now

読み方のコツ

経済関連の記事では、いろいろなデータがよく使われます。過去からの推移について述べる記事では、数値や年号などに注意しましょう。

Post-reading tasks

A 本文の内容をもとにして以下のグラフを完成させましょう。

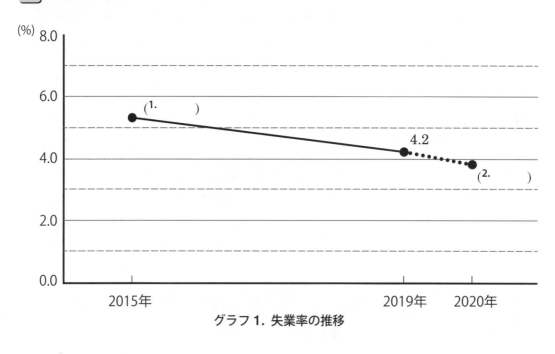

グラフ1. 失業率の推移

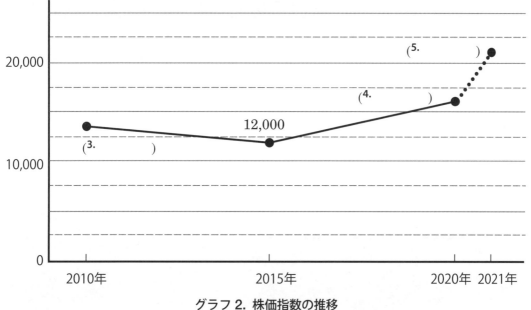

グラフ2. 株価指数の推移

B 次の各文が本文の内容に合っていれば T、間違っていれば F を（　）に記入しましょう。
また、その根拠となった本文中の文に下線を引きましょう。

1. (　) The professor posted the company's fiscal report for the year on a daily blog yesterday.
2. (　) Last year, the wage growth rate was higher than in 2015.
3. (　) The unemployment rate will decrease by half this year in comparison to last year.
4. (　) Kato thinks the stock market index will drop by the end of next year.
5. (　) The Japanese economy could be damaged by the negative effects of inflation next year.

C

1. 音声を聞き、空所を数字で埋めましょう。　DL 62　CD 62

University Students Say No More Books

The NFUCA* reported that a majority of university students in Japan do not read books. In 2007, (1.　　)% of the students said they did not read books. In 2012, it was (2.　　)%. However, the report concluded that the number reached (3.　　)% in 2017.

*NFUCA: 全国大学生活協同組合連合会（National Federation of University Co-operative Associations）

2. 1の内容を折れ線グラフにしてみましょう。

Percentage of university students who do not read books

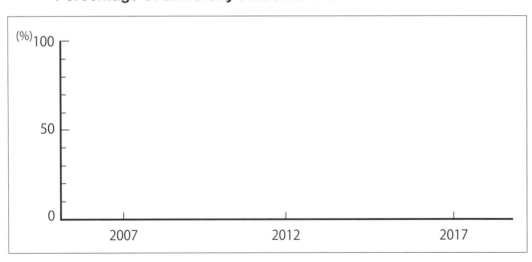

UNIT 15

Not Hearing a Gorilla

報告する（科学）

このユニットでは、脳に関する実験レポートを通して、科学のレポートの文体に慣れ、発見を報告する方法を学びます。

🫘 Pre-reading tasks

A 自分の意見に合うものを［　］から選ぶか（　）に記入して、質問に答えましょう。

Q1. Do you think that science has made our life better?　▶ **[Yes. / No.]**

Q2. What was your favorite subject in high school?
▶ My favorite subject in high school was **[English / science / art /
(　　　　　　)]**.

B **A** の Q1〜2 について、クラスメイトの意見を聞いてみましょう。

	Peer #1 Name: _____	Peer #2 Name: _____
Q1.	☐ Yes. ☐ No.	☐ Yes. ☐ No.
Q2.	☐ English　☐ science ☐ art　　　☐ (　　　　　　)	☐ English　☐ science ☐ art　　　☐ (　　　　　　)

67

Reading

次の英文を読みましょう（太字は本 Unit の重要語句です）。

Not Hearing a Gorilla

1 In a famous **experiment**, people are asked to watch a video and count the number of times that basketballs are passed from one person to another. Half of the **viewers** do not see a gorilla that appears and walks slowly across the screen. Although their eyes see the gorilla and their brains **receive** the image, the viewers do not have any memory of the gorilla. Researchers believe the brain ignores the gorilla because it is not expected to be seen and its appearance is not helpful in **completing** the basketball-counting task.

2 A group of scientists who study how the brain understands sounds wondered if the brain could also ignore **obvious** sounds that are not expected to be heard and not helpful in completing a task. To prepare for their experiment they **recorded** two conversations. In one, two men talk with each other as they prepare food for a party. In the other conversation, two women talk as they wrap gifts for the same party. The test subjects were told to follow either the men's conversation or the women's. They wore headphones and listened to the conversations, which were played at the same time. In the middle of the conversations a different, male voice said, "I'm a gorilla" sixteen times.

3 After listening to the conversations, the volunteers answered questions about the one they had followed. When asked if they heard any strange **statements**, almost none of those who followed the women's conversation heard the **phrase** "I'm a gorilla." As for those who followed the men's conversations, two out of three heard the phrase. Since this group **paid attention to** the male voices, it is not surprising that they were more likely to hear the gorilla statement. Even so, the study results add to the **evidence** that concentrating on a task may cause us to miss strange things that are happening around us.

Notes

l. 6: ignore「〜を無視する」　l. 13: wrap「〜を包む」　l. 22: more likely to「〜する傾向が強い、〜しがちである」

UNIT 15 Not Hearing a Gorilla

読み方のコツ

科学的な実験レポートを読む際には、「目的」、「方法」、「結果」、そして「考察」という文章構成に注意するとよいでしょう。

Post-reading tasks

A 本文の内容をもとにして以下の表を完成させましょう。

実験目的	脳が、予期されず、そして、課題遂行に無意味な音声を(1.　　　　)のかどうかを明らかにすること
実験方法	① 2つの会話を同時に流す 　　A: 2人の(2.　　　　)の会話 　　B: 2人の(3.　　　　)の会話 ② どちらか一方の会話に集中して聞くように指示する ③ 会話の途中で違う男性の声で「(4.　　　　)」と流す
結果	(3.　　　　)の会話を聞くグループは、「(4.　　　　)」という声に気がつかなかったが、(2.　　　　)の会話を聞くグループには、「(4.　　　　)」という声に気がついた人がいた

B 次の各文が本文の内容に合っていればT、間違っていればFを(　　)に記入しましょう。また、その根拠となった本文中の文に下線を引きましょう。

1. (　) Half of the video viewers do not have any memory of the gorilla because their brains don't receive its image.

2. (　) In a recorded conversation, two men talk with each other as they wrap gifts for a party.

3. (　) During the experiment, the subjects were asked to wear headphones.

4. (　) It was easier for those who listened to the men's conversation to notice the strange statements.

5. (　) Our brains are able to automatically select information that's needed for completing given tasks.

C

1. 以下のテーマから1つを選び、下の(1)〜(3)の観点について、Presentation tips を参考に英語でプレゼンテーションをしてみましょう。選択肢以外のテーマを選んでもかまいません。

   - The country I want to visit（行ってみたい国）
   - The thing I want to buy（欲しいもの）
   - The thing I want to try while I am a student（学生時代にやってみたいこと）

   (1) Why do you want to (visit the country / buy it / try it)?
   (2) What do you keep doing in order to achieve it?
   (3) What will happen after achieving it?

   Presentation tips

   - I would like to (visit / buy / try) _____ .
     (1) It is because _____ .
     (2) In order to achieve my goal, I keep (studying / exercising / checking / …) ….
     (3) After achieving it, I will be more (confident in / satisfied with / positive about / …) ….

2. クラスメイトのプレゼンテーションを聞いて、以下に内容を記録しましょう。

   Name: _____

   - He/She wants to (visit / buy / try) _____ .

(1) Why does he/she want to (visit the country / buy it / try it)?
(2) What does he/she keep doing in order to achieve it?
(3) What will happen after achieving it?

本書には音声CD（別売）があります

English Stream: Elementary
インプットからアウトプットへ：初級編

2019年1月20日　初版第1刷発行
2024年2月20日　初版第7刷発行

編著者　　竹　内　　　理
　　　　　住　　政二郎
　　　　　薮　越　知　子
　　　　　植　木　美千子
　　　　　Brent Cotsworth

発行者　　福　岡　正　人
発行所　　株式会社　金星堂
（〒101-0051）東京都千代田区神田神保町3-21
　　　　　Tel. (03) 3263-3828（営業部）
　　　　　　　(03) 3263-3997（編集部）
　　　　　Fax (03) 3263-0716
　　　　　http://www.kinsei-do.co.jp

編集担当　西田碧　　　　　　　Printed in Japan
印刷所・製本所／株式会社カシヨ

本書の無断複製・複写は著作権法上での例外を除き禁じられています。本書を代行業者等の第三者に依頼してスキャンやデジタル化することは、たとえ個人や家庭内での利用であっても認められておりません。
落丁・乱丁本はお取り替えいたします。
ISBN978-4-7647-4079-2　　C1082